GBC@50

GBC@50

A unique insight into fifty years of

THE GAELIC BOOKS COUNCIL

THE GAELIC BOOKS COUNCIL

Published by The Gaelic Books Council, 32 Mansfield Street, Glasgow G11 5QP Scotland

First published 2018
© The Gaelic Books Council 2018

Written and edited by Mairi MacCuish and John Storey.
Introduction by Catriona Murray.
The Gaelic Books Council is grateful for permission to reproduce photographs and extracts from other materials.
All rights reserved.

Book and cover design by River Design, Reston, Scotland.
Printed and bound by Gwasg Gomer, Llandysul, Ceredigion, Wales.

The Gaelic Books Council is grateful to the Scottish Government for assistance towards the publication of this book.

A CIP catalogue record for this title is available from the British Library.

lage / isbn: 9780951281093

A Gaelic edition of this publication is available.
ISBN 9780951281086

www.gaelicbooks.org

CONTENTS

FOREWORD

In recognition of fifty years of support for Scottish Gaelic publishing, the Gaelic Books Council has produced this short guide to the organisation's history and activities.

This booklet is merely an introduction to the Gaelic Books Council: the comprehensive, definitive account has yet to be written. Nevertheless, we hope this small publication will provide the reader with an insight into how the organisation, and indeed Gaelic literature and publishing, has developed over the past five decades.

John Storey and Mairi MacCuish, September 2018

ACKNOWLEDGMENTS

We are grateful to everyone who assisted with information and material for this publication, in particular Ian MacDonald.

We would like to thank the following for the provision of images:

Tim Armstrong; Ronald Black; Kevin Bree; Julie Broadfoot – juliebee.co.uk; Angus Peter Campbell; Myles Campbell; Màiri Sìne Campbell; CLÀR; Comhdháil Náisiúnta na Gaeilge; Liam Crouse; Anna Deplano - graficanna.com; Rody Gorman; Sandy Jones; Ian MacDonald; Alasdair MacLeod and The Daily Record (photo of The Gaelic Books Council at the Scottish Gaelic Awards 2017); Calum L. MacLeod; Murdo MacLeod Photographer – murdophoto.com (Finlay MacLeod at Word 2008); Jessie Anne Matthew and the Scottish National Gallery of Modern Art (Iain Crichton Smith); Seonag Monk; Marie C. Macaulay; Dolina MacLennan; Margaret Anne MacLeod, Acair Ltd; Maureen Macleod; Niall O'Gallagher; Scottish Book Trust (Mòrag Law, Marion F. Morrison and Sheena MacGregor); Roddy Simpson, photographer (Derick Thomson); Willie Urquhart, West Highland Free Press.

INTRODUCTION

My association with the Gaelic Books Council goes back to the 1980s, when I was a student in the Celtic Department of the University of Glasgow where the organisation was based. As Editorial Officer at the Books Council, Ian MacDonald was a key member of the staff within the Department and I was fortunate to be given the opportunity to work with Ian for a short period in 1986, following my graduation. I remember with fondness the morning and afternoon tea-breaks, during which I developed an insight into the dynamic and etiquette of the academic staffroom. When I did a post-graduate diploma in publishing at the University of Stirling, I was grateful for the support and encouragement I received from Ian and from Professor Derick Thomson.

I first served as a member of the board of the Books Council from 1994-1997 and I am honoured to be its Chair in this landmark 50th year. The Gaelic Books Council is the leading global organisation for the support of Gaelic writing and publishing. Long may it continue!

Catriona Murray, Chair, September 2018

Professor Derick Thomson, Chair, 1968-91.

THE GAELIC BOOKS COUNCIL: 1969–1978

The Gaelic Books Council (GBC) – or An Comann Leabhraichean, as it was originally known in Gaelic – was established at the University of Glasgow on 20th December 1968 with Professor Derick Thomson, Department of Celtic, as Chair. The organisation was set up with the specific purpose of supporting the publication of Gaelic books. The Council received modest funding from the Scottish Education Department, as well as the Scottish Arts Council and the Catherine McCaig Trust.[1]

In 1969, John Murray joined the organisation as Editorial Officer and its first member of staff. He would spend six years with the Council. In the same year *Oirthir Tìm*, by Rev. Colin N. Mackenzie (Gairm Publications, 1969), was the first book to be awarded a GBC publication grant. The Council would go on to fund over 120 books in its first decade. The publications were diverse and, to name but a few, included *Rannan Èibhinn Cloinne* by Màiri Tàilleir (Gairm, 1969), *An Aghaidh Choimheach* by John Murray (Gairm, 1973), *A' Choille Chiar* by Catriona and Morag Montgomery (Clò Beag, 1974) and *Fo Sgàil a' Swastika* by Donald John MacDonald (Club Leabhar, 1974).

Ian MacDonald, Editorial Officer in 1976.

The Gaelic Books Council catalogue, first issue, 1975.

Support for publishers was considered vital, and in 1977 the Council agreed to contribute to a new initiative in the Western Isles, with an initial plan for the publication of a series of twelve children's books. Acair Ltd is now the largest Gaelic publisher in the world.

The GBC recognised the importance of supporting Gaelic writers in their craft, and in 1975 the first commission grant was allocated, to assist Donald E. Meek in the completion of *Màiri Mhòr nan Òran: Taghadh de a h-Òrain* (Gairm, 1977). In 1976, Ian MacDonald began work as Editorial Officer and would go on to be a mainstay of the organisation for 34 years.

From the outset, the Council was determined to reach out to the community. A comprehensive Gaelic books catalogue was published in 1975, with regular updates over the years, and a variety of people were temporarily employed to sell books across the west coast in the years before the organisation had a full-time Field Officer. Amongst those who took the wheel of the GBC van were individuals who would make a significant impact on Gaelic publishing in later years, including Ronald Black, Donald Meek and Richard Cox. The Gaelic Books Council mobile bookshop became a familiar sight in Gaelic-speaking areas, where often people had no other access to Gaelic literature. However, sales tours were not without incident. On one trip, the van was extensively damaged in a road accident in Harris and had to make the return journey to Glasgow on a lorry!

1. £350 from the Scottish Arts Council, £500 from the Catherine McCaig Trust and £5,000 from the Scottish Education Department.

Ronald Black, 1970. Sales trip to the Western Isles.

1979–1988

The Gaelic Books Council didn't restrict itself to selling in the Highlands and Islands and, from the early 1980s, book sales were regularly held in Edinburgh and even, once a year, in Manchester and London. A new van was bought in 1983, at a cost of £18,000. Towards the end of the decade, however, economic conditions became more challenging and the decision was taken to stop selling door-to-door. In practice, though, GBC Field Officers proceeded to tour with a hired van into the early 1990s.

The Gaelic Books Council van, Manchester, 1978.

Throughout this decade, Derick Thomson continued as Chair and Dolina MacLennan and Ann Matheson became the Books Council's first female Board members, in 1981 and 1986 respectively.

Sandra MacKay, book sale, Royal National Mod, Stornoway, 1979.

The Gaelic Books Council van, Glasgow, 1981.

Dolina MacLennan, Board member, 1981-83.

The Scottish Poetry Library was established in 1984 and the Council donated a copy of every Gaelic poetry book in print. Two years later the GBC again supported the SPL by lending the organisation its mobile bookshop for a poetry tour of communities in the north-east of Scotland.

In 1985, as a result of the University's decision to relocate the Department of Celtic, the Council moved premises for the first time and left 6 Lilybank Gardens for 5 University Gardens.

The GBC funded and attended a successful European conference in Stornoway on Children's Publishing in Lesser Used Languages in 1987. In the years that followed, collaboration increased between Scottish Gaelic publishers and their European counterparts. For example, *Stamh* (Acair, 1991), written by Annie MacDonald, was published in Scottish Gaelic, Irish, Welsh and Faroese. Leabhraichean Beaga published the *Globi agus Tòmas* series in 1996; a collaboration with An Here, a publisher from Brittany.

Despite the Council only having a small staff, writers and publishers continued to be supported. Recipients of GBC commissions included Iain Crichton Smith, Calum Ferguson and Eilidh Watt. Although there were only a handful of active Gaelic publishers, Acair, Gairm and others continued to publish regularly. New companies emerged too, such as Skye-based publisher Taigh na Teud. The Council's 300th publication grant since 1968 was awarded to Acair for *Ruairidh Robot* by John Murray in 1988.

It was the beginning of the move towards the digital age, and in 1988 first consideration was given to buying a word-processor to replace the time-consuming typewriters and Gestetner copier used in the University.

1989–1998

The 1990s was a decade of significant change.

Marie C. Macaulay began work as Secretary in 1990, a post she held for 18 years. She became a familiar public face for the Gaelic Books Council, representing the organisation in many capacities including annual sales events at the Royal National Mod, as well as in the GBC shop in Partick. John Norman MacDonald, Sales and Finance Officer, succeeded Marie following her retirement in 2008.

Derick Thomson chaired his last Council meeting in 1991, after 23 years as head of the organisation. The position was transferred to the incoming Professor of Celtic at Glasgow University, Professor Donald MacAulay. A year later, following detailed discussion by the Board regarding concerns as to the differing interpretations of the word 'Comann', it was agreed to formally change the organisation's Gaelic name to 'Comhairle nan Leabhraichean'. The title is still in use to the present day.

Professor Donald MacAulay, Chair, 1991-96.

Marie C. Macaulay, Secretary, in the GBC's offices at the University of Glasgow, 1990.

John Storey, Development Officer, at the GBC premises at 22 Mansfield Street, 1998.

The Council flitted once again in 1995, briefly to Ivy Lodge, a University building at 63 Gibson Street. In 1996, the Gaelic Books Council became a charitable company with independent status, severing formal ties with the University of Glasgow. The Council moved to a new shop and office at 22 Mansfield Street in Partick. This was the first time the organisation had its own public retail premises.

The same year, with backing from the organisation's main funder, the Scottish Arts Council, the GBC took on further responsibilities in agreeing to manage and promote Cuairt nam Bàrd. The annual Scottish Gaelic-Irish poetry exchange was established in 1971 and, with valuable assistance from Morag MacLeod at the School of Scottish Studies in Edinburgh, it was brought under the direction of the Books Council.

In 1997, John Storey began working at the GBC and the organisation went online with its first website, along with new email and credit card facilities. Other new sales initiatives were developed, such as A' Chiste Leabhraichean, the Gaelic book club.

*The Gaelic Books Council's newly refurbished shop
at 22 Mansfield Street, Partick, 1998.*

*A cake to celebrate the newly updated GBC website, 1998.
Brian Wilson MP (Scottish Office) launched proceedings.*

A' Chiste Leabhraichean, the Gaelic book club for
young people and adults. Second issue, 1998.

Gaelic writers continued to make their mark on Scottish literature in this decade, with Aonghas Dubh MacNeacail winning the Stakis Scottish Writer of the Year Award in 1997.

The GBC bookshop was revamped in 1998, following a successful application to the National Lottery fund, and sponsorship was secured from Balvenie and Glenfiddich Distilleries for its official opening. The first book to be launched in the new shop was *Keino*, the seminal Gaelic novel by Norman Maclean.

Publishing novels in Scottish Gaelic was still a relatively rare occurence but that would soon change.

Angus Peter Campbell, Norman Campbell, Maggie MacInnes (singer) and Calum Campbell (piper) - Irish Poetry Tour, 2002.

Cuairt nam Bàrd in Scotland, tour poster, September 2004.

1999–2008

During this decade, Gaelic writing in schools was encouraged through projects such as Sgrìobhadh san Sgìre, and community initiatives to stimulate interest in Gaelic books included the Glasgow Gaelic Book Group. John Storey, Development Officer, represented the GBC on a Department of Trade and Industry facilitated marketing tour to Canada in 1999. The DTI itinerary included Toronto, Vancouver and Montreal, where John did his best to sell Gaelic books in the largest city in French-speaking Quebec!

The Irish Poetry Tour visited nearly 40 Scottish communities over the period 1999-2008, with reciprocal visits to Ireland. From 2004 onwards, the tour was organised by Mairi MacCuish, the newly-appointed Outreach and Editorial Officer. This was the first time the GBC had four full-time members of staff. Scottish Gaelic poets who participated in the Tour during the GBC's tenure included Meg Bateman, Rody Gorman, Maletta MacPhail and Christopher Whyte.

The 700th title to receive GBC support - *Ecstasy agus Sgeulachdan Eile* by Ré Ó Laighléis (CLÀR) - was published in 2004. An impressive landmark, but there was concern about the low number of Gaelic publishers. In 2002, according to Board minutes, the shortage of publishers was the worst in memory. *Gairm* magazine ceased that same year after 200 issues, and Skye-based Cànan Ltd stopped publishing in 2007.

During the National Mod in Stornoway in 2005, news was received of a fire at the premises of Gairm Publications at 29 Waterloo Street, Glasgow. A year earlier, the Gaelic Books Council had taken over the remaining stock of Gairm titles, moving most of it to the GBC store. Sadly, the fire resulted in the demolition of the Waterloo Street building, and with it the copies of *Gairm* magazine still in storage there were lost.

Despite such fragility, sales of Gaelic books flourished. In 2005-06, the Gaelic Books Council recorded annual sales of £103,706: an unsurpassed figure. The Scottish Arts Council expressed its confidence in the GBC and granted 'Foundation' funding status to the organisation in 2006.

Contributing to the retail success was a new publishing venture co-ordinated by John Storey: Ùr-Sgeul. Described by Moray Watson as "bringing changes of seismic proportions in the publishing of Gaelic prose," the Ùr-Sgeul imprint, published by CLÀR, propelled the novel to the forefront of the Gaelic literary canon.[2] Authors received national recognition for the quality of their work, with Angus Peter Campbell's debut novel, *An Oidhche Mus Do Sheòl Sinn* voted one of the 'Top Ten Best Scottish Books Ever'.[3] As part of the series, Norma Macleod produced the first Gaelic trilogy for adults, comprising *Dìleas Donn* (2006), *Taingeil Toilichte* (2008) and *Suthainn Sìor* (2011).

Short stories also featured strongly, with the imprint providing a platform for a new generation of writers including Tim Armstrong, Alison Lang and Mairi E. Macleod. Ùr-Sgeul combined key features: bold subject-matter, high quality production and consistently innovative marketing.

The GBC recognised that in order for such momentum to continue, regular, professional support for new authors would be crucial.

2. Moray Watson, *An Introduction to Gaelic Fiction* (Edinburgh University Press, 2011), p.145.

3. The List Magazine (Edinburgh, 2005).

Dr Finlay MacLeod, launch of Dìomhanas *(Ùr-Sgeul/CLÀR),*
Word Festival, University of Aberdeen, 2008.

Mairi E. MacLeod, launch of A' Ghlainne agus Sgeulachdan Eile
(Ùr-Sgeul/CLÀR), Portree, 2010.

2009–2018

The Gaelic New Writers Awards, launched with Scottish Book Trust in 2009, proved a vital stepping-stone, with several recipients becoming established authors, including Maureen Macleod, Niall O'Gallagher and Sandy Jones. Other new initiatives included the Gaelic Playwright Award (with Playwrights' Studio Scotland) and the Gaelic Young Writer Award (with Scottish Book Trust). The Donald Meek Award was established in 2010, with support from Bòrd na Gàidhlig and Creative Scotland. The competition plays a crucial role in developing new work, given that it is only open to previously unpublished writing.

In 2010, Rosemary Ward succeeded Ian MacDonald as Director, and the Gaelic Books Council relocated to 32 Mansfield Street, where the organisation's shop, offices and store-rooms were finally all within the same building. A full-time Sales and Marketing Officer, Shelagh Campbell, was appointed that year.

Iain MacRae (winner) and Eoghan Stewart (second place),
The Donald Meek Award, 2017.

Leugh is Seinn le Linda: Linda MacLeod, the Gaelic Books Council shop, 2017.

Following the departure of Ian MacDonald, who had done so much editorial work over the years, the GBC prioritised the development of Gaelic editorial skills in collaboration with language specialist Roddy MacLean. A suite of courses, accredited by Glasgow Caledonian University, focusing on orthography and grammar from an editorial perspective, proved attractive not just to publishing professionals but within the media and education sectors too.

The Ùr-Sgeul series came to an end in 2013, but GBC support for fiction continued through 'Aiteal' (Acair) and the 'Ficsean Luath' (Luath Press) imprints. Between 2014-17, Sandstone Press published 12 titles in the 'Lasag' series (building on their earlier 'Meanmnach' imprint), aimed at the increasingly important adult learners' market. CLÀR continued to publish key titles, as well as launching *STEALL*, a new Gaelic magazine in 2016.

Under the direction of Rosemary Ward, the Gaelic Books Council was involved in a number of new initiatives, particularly with regard to encouraging children to read, for example Read, Write, Count in partnership with the Scottish Government. The Leugh is Seinn le Linda project, established in 2015, supported younger readers and their families to access and enjoy Gaelic books and prompted a BBC Alba television series, while the GBC-sponsored Giglets project provided new e-resources for children. Towards the end of the decade, the GBC began to collaborate with Scottish Book Trust on the annual Book Bug series, and provided an advisory role to the First Minister's Reading Challenge.

With five full-time staff and an ambitious remit, the Gaelic Books Council has cemented its reputation as the lead organisation for Scottish Gaelic literature.

Mòrag Law and Marion F. Morrison, recipients of the Gaelic New Writers Awards, 2017.

John Norman MacDonald, Mairi MacCuish, Shelagh Campbell, Rosemary Ward and Catriona Murray, at the Scottish Gaelic Awards, 2017.

SUPPORT FOR WRITERS

The Gaelic Books Council has supported numerous authors over the years. In the last decade, as mentioned, initiatives to develop the skills and experience of Gaelic writers have been introduced in collaboration with several national organisations. However, there has been a particular opportunity available to all Gaelic writers for nearly fifty years that is worthy of further attention: the commission grant. Providing funding for authors over an agreed time-frame, a commission grant allows writers, wherever in the world they are based, time and space to pursue their work. Several recipients of commission grants have already been highlighted, and over the next few pages we provide a further sample of those who have received support.

In addition to offering commissions, during the 1970s and 1980s the Council ran a series of competitions to encourage new Gaelic writing. Titles published as a result included Iain Crichton Smith's *Iain am measg nan Reultan* (Gairm, 1970) and Angus Campbell's classic *A' Suathadh ri Iomadh Rubha* (Gairm, 1973).

Although priority is given to original Gaelic work, there has been a willingness to consider projects to translate into Gaelic from other languages. Homer's *Odyssey*, for example, was translated into Gaelic by John MacLean and published by Gairm in 1976, and *Seachd Luinneagan à Shakespeare*, translated by Duncan Gillies, was published in 1988 by the University of Glasgow's Department of Celtic. Among many others, *Kidnapped*, *The Little Prince* and several books from the *Asterix* and *Tintin* series have been versioned into Scottish Gaelic with the support of the GBC.

IAIN CRICHTON SMITH
The renowned, prolific author was
supported at many stages by the GBC.
Here he is at home in 1980.

CALUM FERGUSON
Calum has written several classics.
Pictured in 1983, the publication year
of *Suileabhan* (Gairm).

ANNE LORNE GILLIES
The author of a range of outstanding
works. Pictured in the early 1980s,
she wrote several children's titles.

MYLES CAMPBELL
Myles c. 1980, the year his debut
poetry collection *Eileanan*
(University of Glasgow) appeared.

SEONAG MONK
Seonag doesn't just write novels!
Pictured c. 1996, the year she wrote
kids' classic *Dòmhnall Phàdraig* (Acair).

DUNCAN GILLIES
From Ness, Duncan is a superb short
story writer. He has produced three
acclaimed collections, published
by CLÀR.

RODY GORMAN
A prolific poet, editor and translator,
Rody hails from Dublin. He lives on
the Isle of Skye.

CATRIONA LEXY CAMPBELL
Novels, drama, radio, TV, short
stories – to name but a few.
Here she is in 2006.

MARY ANNE MACDONALD
The author of the novel *Cleas Sgàthain* (Ùr-Sgeul/CLÀR, 2008), she has also published work for teenagers.

NORMAN CAMPBELL
Novelist, poet, author of children's books, Norman (1942-2015) set consistently high standards.

ANGUS PETER CAMPBELL
Angus Peter's award-winning titles include *An Oidhche Mus Do Sheòl Sinn, Aibisidh* and *Memory and Straw*.

NIALL O'GALLAGHER
Niall has produced two poetry collections, *Beatha Ùr* (2013) and *Suain nan Trì Latha* (2016), both published by CLÀR.

SANDY JONES
In 2011, Sandy won a place on
the Gaelic New Writers Awards.
Her poetry is published by Acair.

MAUREEN MACLEOD
Novelist and travel writer Maureen,
from Ness, was also a recipient of a
Gaelic New Writers Award in 2011.

CALUM L. MACLEOD
Calum in 2017, the year his debut
novel, *A' Togail an t-Srùbain*, was
published by CLÀR.

SHEENA MACGREGOR
Sheena, from Edinburgh, was
awarded the Gaelic Young Writer
('What's Your Story?') Award in 2017.

Ian MacDonald and a representative from the Scottish Qualifications Authority (SQA), at the launch of GOC 2, 2005.

Since its inception, the Gaelic Books Council has been at the forefront of Gaelic language development, and numerous authors have benefited from advice on orthography and grammar. *Gaelic Orthographic Conventions* (GOC) first appeared in 1981 and is widely held as the definitive standard for modern Gaelic spelling. Although officially representing the University of Glasgow, GBC Chair Professor Derick Thomson was on the GOC advisory panel at the time. Ian MacDonald was one of the advisors to *Gaelic Orthographic Conventions 2* (SQA, 2005), and again when a bilingual version of GOC 2 was published in 2009.

The Gaelic Books Council has always acknowledged the importance of public recognition for Gaelic writers. Literature Day at the Royal National Mod was first provided with financial support from the GBC in 1995, and since 2013 the Council has produced *Lasair Litreachais*, an annual booklet featuring the work of the main literary prize-winners.

The GBC has endeavoured to ensure Gaelic authors are afforded equal recognition within the wider Scottish literary landscape, and throughout the years support and guidance have been provided to various organisations. Ian MacDonald acted as an advisor to the Saltire Society Literary Awards for many years, and in 2003 Martin MacIntyre became the first Gaelic author to win the First Book of the Year Award for *Ath-Aithne* (Ùr-Sgeul/CLÀR, 2003).

Since then, other Gaelic winners at the Saltire Awards include Tim Armstrong, winner of the First Book of the Year Award in 2013, for his Gaelic science fiction novel *Air Cuan Dubh Drilseach* (CLÀR), and Peter Mackay with Iain S. MacPherson, editors of *An Leabhar Liath / The Light Blue Book* (Luath Press) for Research Book of the Year in 2017.

Other GBC supported literary awards include the Wigtown Poetry Competition and Glasgow University Ossianic Society's Gaelic writing prizes.

The following authors are past recipients of the premier annual Gaelic literary prize, The Donald Meek Award: Finlay MacLeod (2010), Margaret Callan (2011), Moray Watson (2012), Martin MacIntyre (2013), Norma Macleod (2014), Alasdair Campbell (2015), Peter Mackay and Iain S. MacPherson (2016), and Iain MacRae (2017).

Individual book launches were relatively rare from the 1970s to the 1990s, but there have been notable exceptions. *The Companion to Gaelic Scotland* was launched by Gairm at the University of Glasgow in 1983. Ten years later, the success of the early Gaelic-Irish Poetry Tour was marked through publication of *Sruth na Maoile* (Canongate/Coiscéim) at an event at the Irish President's official residence, Áras an Uachtaráin in Dublin. Acair launched – almost literally – Calum Ferguson's *Hiort* on a Caledonian MacBrayne ferry in Stornoway in 1995.

Since 2003 and the start of Ùr-Sgeul, Gaelic book launches and author events have increased in prominence. The Council forged strong links with Edinburgh International Book Festival and this has allowed Gaelic authors to grace the stage of the world's largest celebration of writers and writing. More recently, the Council has collaborated with Aye Write! in Glasgow, Imprint in Ayrshire, the Ullapool Book Festival and the Nairn Book Festival, amongst others. The Royal National Mod continues to provide a platform for Gaelic book launches, and events are regularly held at the GBC shop in Partick.

Nowadays, technology provides new opportunities to forge links with Gaelic communities no matter the distance. For example, 2018 has seen the establishment of a web forum for Gaelic readers, as well as the online reading group, Leugh Leam, which facilitates discussion of Gaelic books, bringing readers together from North Uist to New York.

Tim Armstrong, winner of the Saltire Society First Book of the Year Award 2013 (for the Gaelic sci-fi novel Air Cuan Dubh Drilseach*). Pictured with John Burnside at the Awards ceremony at the Mitchell Library, Glasgow.*

*Agnes Rennie, Donalda Riddell and Margaret Anne MacLeod of Acair,
marking the company's 40th anniversary in 2017.*

SUPPORT FOR PUBLISHERS

Since 1968, over 1,000 Gaelic and Gaelic-related books have been funded by the Gaelic Books Council through publication grants. The Council has supported many kinds of Gaelic books, including poetry, fiction, biography, drama, politics, music, religion, children's stories, research, and learning materials. In a short volume such as this, it would be impossible to focus on every significant publication; there have been so many remarkable books. In addition to titles already mentioned, we provide a brief selection over the next few pages.

A range of publishers have been involved in this work. Some are no longer active, such as Gairm Publications, arguably the most important Gaelic publisher of the 20th Century. In addition to *Gairm* magazine, the company published approximately 120 individual titles over fifty years. Derick Thomson (along with Finlay J. MacDonald)

GAIRM - Aireamh 200 *(Gairm Publications)*
– *the final issue, 2002.*

was instrumental in establishing the company and played a huge role in Gairm's success over the years. The final Gairm title, *Ainmeil an Eachdraidh*, edited by Thomson, appeared in 1997.

Other publishers have come and gone, including Club Leabhar, An t-Eileanach, Macdonald Publishers, Clò-Beag, Clò Chailleann, Crùisgean and Druim Fraoich, but they left behind a precious legacy.

Nowadays, the Gaelic Books Council works with publishers such as Acair, Leabhraichean Beaga, CLÀR, Taigh na Teud, Clann Tuirc and Dealan-Dè. Acair celebrated their 40th anniversary in 2017, and have published several hundred Gaelic titles (in addition to their English language output). Notable Acair publications – there are too many to mention – include *Fonn* (2013), a beautiful, substantial celebration of the musical talents of the Campbells of Greepe, as well as *Rònan agus Brianuilt* by Finlay MacLeod, Acair's first children's book, published in 1978 and reprinted to celebrate the anniversary.

Over the years, predominantly English-language publishers have also received support for Gaelic titles. Canongate, for example, published a number of GBC-assisted Gaelic books from the 1980s into the early part of this century, including *Nua-Bhàrdachd Ghàidhlig* edited by Donald MacAulay (1987) and *An Leabhar Mòr: The Great Book of Gaelic* (2002). Birlinn produced several notable Gaelic titles including *Songs of Gaelic Scotland* by Anne Lorne Gillies (2005), and *Duanaire na Sracaire,* edited by Wilson McLeod and Meg Bateman (2007). Publishers from abroad such as Coiscéim in Ireland and, more recently, Bradan Press in Nova Scotia, have also benefited from GBC funding.

Different formats have been encouraged over the years. One of the first Gaelic audio publications, *Ceòl na Gàidhlig* - a selection of poetry and song - was published in cassette form by Scotsoun in 1975. As technology changed, the Gaelic Books Council took note and encouraged publishers to try new approaches. In 2006, CLÀR, publishers of Ùr-Sgeul, were praised by the late Dr Gavin Wallace of the Scottish Arts Council for being ahead of most other publishers in Scotland with their use of video and DVD technology. Today, specialist and digital publications, as well as more conventional formats, continue to receive support.

*Martin MacIntyre with Dr Gavin Wallace of the Scottish Arts Council,
at the launch of the first Ùr-Sgeul catalogue, 2004.*

In addition to assistance with the practical costs of production, GBC
publication grants allow publishers to employ professional Gaelic
editors and proof-readers, helping to ensure written excellence in
Gaelic texts. It is a source of encouragement that new Gaelic editors
are being supported through GBC training initiatives such as those
developed in conjunction with Roddy MacLean.

To safeguard the future of Gaelic literature, a new generation of Gaelic
publishers is vital. In recent years, training for new entrants to the
industry has been a priority, and since 2012 the GBC has offered a
funded scholarship for Gaelic speakers wishing to undertake an MLitt
in Publishing Studies at the University of Stirling. Additional advice
and assistance is also available to new Gaelic publishers working on
their first book.

Finally, we must acknowledge that whilst support from organisations
such as the Gaelic Books Council is important, it is the spirit and
determination of a select band of individuals that has been the driving
force for many of the key Gaelic publishing achievements. Often at
personal expense, these individuals have worked tirelessly to bring some
of the most important works of Scottish Gaelic literature to fruition.

Liam Crouse, recipient of a Gaelic Books Council scholarship for MLitt Publishing Studies, University of Stirling, 2012-13.

The Gaelic Books Council is indebted to everyone involved in Gaelic publishing over the last 50 years – writers, publishers and readers – and we look forward to working with the next generation.

"1968 is rightly remembered as the year of radical uprisings against injustice. Students demonstrated on the streets of Paris and in other cities across the world. There were large-scale protests in the United States against racism and for civil rights. In that same year, a further radical step was taken when the Gaelic Books Council was established. In the midst of a cultural climate that showed very little support, indeed hostility, towards Scottish Gaelic, we might acknowledge the formation of the Gaelic Books Council as yet another courageous and visionary fight for rights. Fifty years later we can be very grateful for, and proud of, that moment in our Gaelic history, and celebrate that the organisation is going strong. The Gaelic Books Council contributes to the enrichment of Scotland's rich cultural and linguistic tapestry and it deserves our support."

Dr Sìm Innes, Rannsachadh na Gàidhlig conference,
University of Edinburgh, 2018

The following pages illustrate a small selection of Gaelic titles supported by the Gaelic Books Council over the years.

An Aghaidh Choimheach
Iain Moireach

1973
An Aghaidh Choimheach / John Murray / Gairm Publications / short stories

SPAGAN
agus am bike ùr

1977

Spàgan agus am Bike Ùr / Ellen Blance and Ann Cook / Longman | Pròiseact Foghlam Dà-chànanach / children

1978
Rònan agus Brianuilt /
Finlay MacLeod / Acair / children

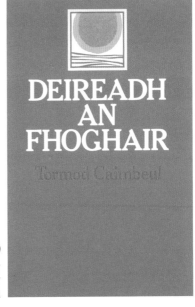

1979
Deireadh an Fhoghair /
Norman Campbell /
W. and R. Chambers / novel

1981

Raonaid / Chrissie Dick /
Clò Chailleann / teenage

1983

Mìcheal agus Niall aig a' chladach /
Lisa Storey / Leabhraichean Beaga / children

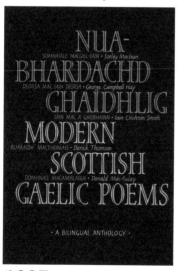

1987

Nua-Bhàrdachd Ghàidhlig /
Donald MacAulay (Editor) / Canongate /
poetry

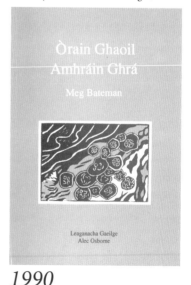

1990

Òrain Ghaoil / *Amhráin Ghrá* /
Meg Bateman / Coiscéim / poetry

AN SGAILE DHORCHA

Iain MacLeòid

1992
An Sgàile Dhorcha / Iain MacLeod / Gairm Publications / teenage

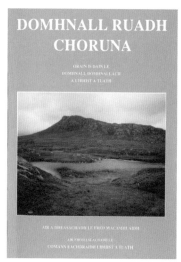

1995

Dòmhnall Ruadh Chorùna / Fred Macaulay
(Editor) / Comann Eachdraidh Uibhist a
Tuath / poetry and song

1996

Gaelic Proverbs / Alexander Nicolson
(Editor) / Birlinn / vocabulary

1998

Keino / Norman Maclean /
Clò Loch Abair / novel

2003

An Oidhche Mus Do Sheòl Sinn /
Angus Peter Campbell / Ùr-Sgeul/CLÀR
/ novel

Litir à Ameireagaidh

Flòraidh NicDhòmhnaill

2007

Litir à Ameireagaidh / Flora MacDonald / Meanmnach/Sandstone Press / novella

Deilbh is Faileasan

Dàin le Domhnall MacAmhlaigh

Images and Reflections   Poems by Donald MacAulay

2008
Deilbh is Faileasan / Donald MacAulay / Acair / poetry

AN
CLAIGEANN
AIG
damien
hirst
AGUS SGEULACHDAN EILE

2009

An Claigeann aig Damien Hirst agus Sgeulachdan Eile / Various writers /
Ùr-Sgeul/CLÀR / short stories

2010

An Tractar agus an Liobht /
Catriona Black / Acair / children

2011

San Dùthaich Ùir / Alison Lang /
Meanmnach/Sandstone / novella

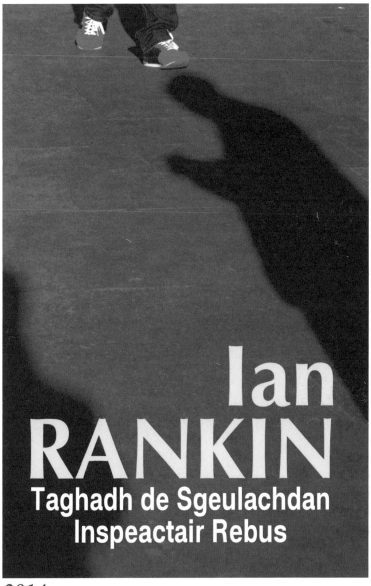

Ian
RANKIN
Taghadh de Sgeulachdan
Inspeactair Rebus

2014

Taghadh de Sgeulachdan Inspeactair Rebus / Ian Rankin / Grace Note Publications / short stories

Iasad Rann

A Borrowing of Verses

Original Gaelic poems and translations
by John Maclean

EDITED BY

William Gillies AND Donald E. Meek

2018

GAELIC BOOKS COUNCIL: STAFF AND BOARD

Whilst every effort has been made to ensure the details for staff and Board members are correct, any mistakes are, of course, entirely the responsibility of the Gaelic Books Council. We do apologise if there are any inaccuracies or ommissions.

Staff are listed chronologically, with a separate section for temporary workers.

In the case of any staff or Board member returning to the GBC, details of their subsequent term(s) of office are located alongside their first entry.

STAFF

John Murray (1969-75) – Editorial Officer

Christine Morrison (1969-70) – Secretary

Mary Ann MacLeod (1971-75) – Secretary

Mairi Trawber (1975) – Secretary

Ian MacLeod (1975-76) – Editorial Officer (part-time)

Sandra MacKay (1975-80) – Secretary

Neil Mitchison (1976-77) – Field Officer

Ian MacDonald (1976-2010) – Editorial Officer; Director

Calum Laing (1978) Field Officer

Tommy Fraser† (1979) – Field Officer

Kathleen MacLeod (1980-85) – Secretary

Metta MacLeod (1981-84) – Field Officer

Colin MacLean† (1984-85) – Field Officer

Joan MacKinnon (1985-86) – Secretary

Catherine Anderson (1986-90) – Secretary

Catriona Murray (1986) – Editorial Officer (part-time)

Kenneth Smith (1986-87) – Field Officer

Chrisella MacKenzie (Ross)† (1987-88) – Field Officer

Fearchar MacLennan (1988-90) – Field Officer

Marie C. Macaulay (1990-2008) – Secretary

Karen Marshalsay (1991-92) – Field Officer

Joetta Macleod (1995) – Outreach Officer

John Storey (1997-present) – Development Officer; Project Officer; Head of Literature and Publishing

Mairi MacCuish (2004-present) – Outreach and Editorial Officer; Literature and Publishing Officer

John Norman MacDonald (2008-present) – Sales and Finance Officer

Rosemary Ward (2010-18) – Director

Shelagh Campbell (2010-12) (2016-present) – Sales and Marketing Officer

Maria MacInnes (2012-13) – Sales and Marketing Officer

Janice Campbell (2014-16) – Sales and Marketing Officer

MOBILE SALES AND OTHER TEMPORARY STAFF

Donald E. Meek (student) – summer sales tour, 1969 (Tiree and Skye)

Ronald Black – summer sales tour, 1970 (Western Isles)

William MacDonald – summer sales tour, 1971 (Uist and Skye)

Duncan MacLaren – summer sales tours, 1970s (Skye and Islay)

Allan MacDonald (student) – summer sales tour, 1973 (Western Isles and Skye)

Neil Mitchison – summer sales tours, 1974 and 1975

Alasdair Duncan† – sales tours, 1975

Elizabeth MacPherson – summer sales tour, 1979 (Barra and Eriskay)

Richard A.V. Cox – Easter sales tour, 1980 (Uist)

Phyllis Wightman – sales tour, 1980 (Uist and Barra)

Sharron Gunn – summer sales tour, 1981 (Colonsay, Mull and Islay)

Alan Boyd (student) – sales tour, 1982 (Tiree)

Fiona Lyon – summer sales tour, 1991 (Skye)

Fearchar MacLennan – sales tours, 1991 (Arran), 1993 (South Uist)

James Galbraith – Saturday shop assistant, 1997

Scott MacDonald – Saturday shop assistant, 1997-98

Faye MacLean – shop and office assistant, 2001-02

Raymond Buchanan – shop assistant, early 2000s

Margaret MacLeod (ex-Gairm) – shop assistant, 2004-05

Dolly Grimmer – shop assistant, 2005-06

Tia Thomson – project co-ordinator, Sgrìobhadh san Sgìre, Highland Region, 2009

Ruaraidh MacIntyre – Saturday shop assistant, 2010

Garry Cooke – shop and store assistant, 2013-16

In addition, placements were arranged in collaboration with Comunn na Gàidhlig, Sabhal Mòr Ostaig, secondary schools and other institutions, in order that students could gain work experience at the Gaelic Books Council premises in Mansfield Street.

CHAIRPERSONS

Professor Derick Thomson*† - Chair (1968-91)

Professor Donald MacAulay*† - Chair (1991-96), member (1968-91)

Boyd Robertson - Chair (1996-2000), member (1992-96)

Donalda MacKinnon - Chair (2000-02), member (2000)

Professor Donald E. Meek - Chair (2002-04), member (2002; 2005-06)

Dr Martin MacGregor - Chair (2005), member (2000-05)

Professor Rob Ó Maolalaigh - Chair (2005-09)

Donald-Iain Brown - Chair (2010-17)

Catriona Murray - Chair (2017-present), member (1994-97)

* in attendance at the first meeting of the Gaelic Books Council

† deceased

BOARD MEMBERS

In the early years, the GBC board was required to include representatives of the Universities of Glasgow, Aberdeen and Edinburgh, as well as An Comunn Gàidhealach.

Farquhar Gillanders*† (1968-86) – University of Glasgow representative

Professor Kenneth H. Jackson*† (1968-71) – University of Edinburgh representative

Professor Donald MacAulay*† (1968-91) – University of Aberdeen representative; Chair (1991-96)

Donald John MacKay*† (1968-70) – An Comunn Gàidhealach representative

Murdo MacLeod*† (1968-70) (1974-83)

Ronald MacLeod*† (1968-69)

John A. Smith*† (1968-88)

R. MacDonald (1968-76)

A. Skinner (1968-69)

John MacKinnon (1970-73)

Douglas Eadie (1970) – Scottish Arts Council representative

Trevor Royle (1971-79) – Scottish Arts Council representative

Norman Burns† (1971-76) – An Comunn Gàidhealach representative

Donald Archie MacDonald† (1971-93) – University of Edinburgh representative

Dr Finlay MacLeod (1971-77)

Dr John W.M. Bannerman† (1977-89)

Malcolm MacLeod† (1977-80) – An Comunn Gàidhealach representative

Rev. Dr. Roderick MacLeod (1978-86)

Walter Cairns† (1979-96) – Scottish Arts Council representative

Dolina MacLennan (1981-83) – An Comunn Gàidhealach representative

Alick J. MacAskill (1982-92)

Alick M. Morrison† (1982-86)

Neil Mackechnie† (1984-93) – An Comunn Gàidhealach representative

Robert MacDonald (1986-96) – University of Glasgow representative

Donald John MacIver† (1986-92)

Dr Ann Matheson (1986-92)

Roderick MacCuish (1989-94)

William MacDonald (1989-95)

Catriona Dunn (1992-2000)

Rachel McPherson (1992-95)

Boyd Robertson (1992-96); Chair (1996-2000)

Jo MacDonald (1994-96); Vice-Chair (1996-2000)

Roy Pedersen (1994-97)

Catriona Murray (1994-97); Chair (2017-present)

Donald J.F. MacInnes (1996-2000) (2013-16); Vice-Chair (2000-02)

Morag Stewart (1996-2001)

Jenny Brown (1996-99) (2001-02) – Scottish Arts Council representative

John Alick MacPherson† (1998-2003)

Cathy MacDonald (1998-2002)

Sheriff Roderick John Macleod (1998-2001)

Dr Gavin Wallace† (2000-01) (c.2003-13) – Scottish Arts Council/ Creative Scotland representative

William MacDonald (2000-05)

Donalda MacKinnon (2000); Chair (2000-02)

Ishbel Murray (2000-04)

Dr Martin MacGregor (2000-03); Vice-Chair (2003-04); Chair (2005)

Joina MacDonald (2002-07)

Norman E. Macdonald† (2002-07)

Professor Donald E. Meek (2002, 2005-06); Chair (2002-04)

Dr Anne Lorne Gillies (2002-05)

Jenny Attala (2002-c.03) – Scottish Arts Council representative

Dougie MacAulay (2003-08)

Christina Walker (2003-04); Vice-Chair (2005-08)

Myles Campbell (2003-06)

Mairead MacDonald (2005-09)

Mark Wringe (2005-09, 2010); Vice-Chair (2009)

Angela MacEachen (2007-09); Vice-Chair (2010-12)

John Carmichael (2007-12)

Donalda McComb (2007-12)

Calum Ross (2007-12)

Duncan MacQuarrie (2008-13)

Marion Sinclair (2008-13); ex-officio, Publishing Scotland representative (2014-present)

Una MacDonald (2010-17)

Katrina MacIver (2012-15)

Alison Buchanan (2012-13)

Seumas Campbell (2012-present)

Dr Moray Watson (2012-15)

Aly Barr (2013-17) – Creative Scotland representative

Christine MacLeod (2013-15)

Katie Murray (2013-present)

Dr Sìm Innes (2016-present)

Ian Smith (2016-present)

Donald Cameron (2017-present)

Morna Butcher (2017-present)

Margaret MacLeod (2017-present)

Alan Bett (2018-present) – Creative Scotland representative

* in attendance at the first meeting of the Gaelic Books Council

† deceased